T0080011

SILVER ROAD

KAZIM ALI

essays, maps & calligraphies SILVER ROAD

TUPELO PRESS

North Adams, Massachusetts

Silver Road.
Copyright © 2018 Kazim Ali. All rights reserved.

Names: Ali, Kazim, 1971– author.
Title: Silver road : essays, maps & calligraphies / Kazim Ali.
Other titles: Tupelo Press lineage series.
Description: First paperback edition: January 2018. | North Adams,
 Massachusetts : Tupelo Press, [2018] | Series: Tupelo Press lineage series
Identifiers: LCCN 2017049457 | ISBN 9781936797998 (pbk. original : alk. paper)
Classification: LCC PS3601.L375 A6 2018b | DDC 811/.6--dc23

Cover and text designed and composed in Dante and Gill Sans by Ann Aspell.
Cover photograph: "New Ice and Birch Reflections, 2015, Dawn" by John Lehet
(www.lehet.com). All rights reserved, and used with permission.

First paperback edition: January 2018.

Other than brief excerpts for reviews and commentaries, no part of this book may
be reproduced by any means without permission of the publisher. Please address
requests for reprint permission or for course-adoption discounts to:

Tupelo Press
P.O. Box 1767, North Adams, Massachusetts 01247
(413) 664-9611 / editor@tupelopress.org / www.tupelopress.org

Tupelo Press is an award-winning independent literary press that publishes fine
fiction, nonfiction, and poetry in books that are a joy to hold as well as read.
Tupelo Press is a registered 501(c)(3) nonprofit organization, and we rely on public
support to carry out our mission of publishing extraordinary work that may be
outside the realm of the large commercial publishers. Financial donations are
welcome and are tax deductible.

ART WORKS.
arts.gov

Supported in part by an award from
the National Endowment for the Arts

ALSO BY KAZIM ALI

CONTENTS

SILVER ROAD

To walk in the world is to find oneself in a body without papers, not a citizen of anything but breath. And to be oneself is to be alone, to be one and no other. Is it true that we are individuals because we are seen and known by others in relationship to them? Or as Gertrude Stein posited, "I am I because my little dog knows me."

Quantum mechanics says that space is granular, made of pieces, and not only that but there is no infinity—nothing infinitely small, nothing infinitely vast. Cold comfort.

Then who when we wander wanders? And to what home can one ever come?

Who is the one without home, who crosses any border from the place he knew and was known into a place where neither is true?

That silver road is longer than its miles, more fraught and dangerous than any myth could tell, more dehumanizing than any background checks or strip searches could intimate.

And if space is finite, thought is finite, time is finite, then who are we in one place and who are we in the other. Who are we before we leave and who are we after.

JANUARY IS A MONTH WITH
TWO FACES

∽

IN 1953 YOKO ONO WROTE HER FIRST SCORE, called *Secret Piece*. It consisted of a musical staff along with two quarter notes under which was handwritten, "with the accompaniment of the birds singing at dawn." To this was later added one line of typescript: "Decide on the one note you want to play. Play to the following accompaniment: The woods from 5 A.M. to 8 A.M. in summer."

I have heard this piece performed by entire orchestras who tromped into the woods to do it, dew-licked and bleary-eyed, and I have heard this piece performed by an individual singer. I have performed this piece myself.

One could talk about it endlessly—how it answers Cage's *4'33"*, how it turns the art-maker into the audience and vice versa, and so on—but instead of infinite theoretical meanings here are very practical notions: Firstly, there is a marriage between technology and the body in the combination of typescript and handwriting on the score. Secondly, this kind of art depends not on rules or learning but on the focused perception of any

4

untrained solitary listener. And finally and most importantly, of course, is the fact that the typewritten instructions and the handwritten score beneath it are not the same. Which are you meant to follow? Conceptual art—at least for Ono, one of its progenitors—was not an idea-based mode of taking the artist out of the equation but an occasion for more art-making. By making of the writing an art, she lifted any constraint on "realization" of the music, the painting, the film, etc.

It's worth mentioning that although in the beginning Ono did realize her own "instructions," at a certain point she just exhibited the instructions themselves as texts in frames. Now that her work is being shown in retrospectives and one-woman shows, the instructions are again being displayed alongside the realizations, which take the form of recordings, paintings, or objects.

I live in an old house built in 1911. It has not been updated or refurbished. One knows immediately upon entering that one is in an older house with its heavy dark wood doors, fixtures, radiators and built-in bookshelves, hutches, and dressers. You cannot come inside and not feel the temporal remove. The house does not have that blank anonymity of contemporary spaces. Because we bought it from people who'd lived here for fifty years and who'd bought it from the people who built it in 1911, we know its full history. We know what happened to the people who lived in this house.

When I sit on the landing of the staircase which splits in two directions down to the first floor, I know that I hunch down in the same place where the Richards girls hid to listen to the funeral of their father, the house's first owner, which was held in the first floor parlor and which they had been forbidden to attend. When I go up to the yoga practice room on the third floor, I remember that this room used to be one of the dormitories for the students who roomed here in the early part of the century, but that the Schoonmakers who bought the house in 1965 used it as storage space for their camping and hiking equipment.

In this way we are always in context. Charles Olson said he took "the central fact of America to be SPACE," but I think now the central fact of America is ERASURE—erasure of both space and time. In America it is possible to forget which lands belonged to which indigenous nation. It is possible in America for actually existing Native peoples to protest the use of their lands and still be ignored by the American government.

For a long time I have dreamt of Ono's piece. What is one note I could play at any given moment? Poetry; body practices of yoga, dance or running; hiking in the mountains; swimming or floating in the ocean; lying on one's back and gazing in the direction of the moon-lonely moon which does not itself illuminate but reveals illumination: these are all practices that allow one—a human body which lives and dies at devastating speed, you will have to agree—to actually see what locality means, how time unravels. You know you are a body that exists in the physical universe, in a context of mass and energy, which do not convert from one to the other but are themselves the same thing.

In the houses of my extended family I sometimes wonder who I am. I am neither professor nor poet nor lover of anyone. My partner's name is known but many of my family have never met him. Our house, that great yellow and blue oasis on the eastern side of Oberlin, Ohio, is unvisited. When I go home for holidays or visits I feel like a spirit somehow, detached from everything, floating through. But time will cruelly divest us of our contexts throughout our lives and we are constantly supposed to invent new ones or see the relationships that once existed in both past and future tenses.

My queerness does not make me a two-spirited person or make available to me any particular magic. It only reveals better that latent quality of loneliness or aloneness shared by any mortal thing. I have come to believe that this sense of alienation is what opened the door for me to poetry.

Time is ordinary, invented and defined by poets and scientists. Every poet, even those who have not studied physics, suspects that time is a fiction, that it is not real, at least not in the way that we think of it. The traditional Persian New Year begins on the first day of spring. The Jewish New Year begins in the autumn, the sunset of the year. The Muslim calendar year is purely lunar and so its beginning floats throughout the year ungoverned by the sun. I prefer this one of course, because it leads the individual into Ono's conundrum: to choose your note, a note that can shift and change throughout the course of one's own life.

Our new year, the American one, the Western one, is the

Roman one: devoted to Janus, the god who could look in two directions at once, to the past and to the future. Of course, if time bends then there are a million directions at once and fate is not a line or thread but a tapestry, a web, endless and infinite.

It was Einstein who first imagined that the universe was both finite and infinite. No, that's not correct: that it was finite but *had no borders*. As on the Earth which is round, at the farthest point in the universe one might meet oneself.

Ono's score always contradicts itself—which is the sound meant to accompany the one note played? Neither body nor spirit is absolute concept or actuality. Nothing *is*. Even considering that, I do not want to forget myself; I do not want to erase the physical in favor of the spirit nor the spirit in favor of the actual world. I want to live in time and space since if in the actual universe there is neither, then this one minute might be my only chance.

You can choose to exist: you can choose not to be a ghost. I learned at a very young age the myth of Abraham and his son, whom God asked him to sacrifice. But I never knew which role was mine to play: that of Isaac the traumatized son ("But father, where is the ram?") or Ishmael the compliant son ("Do what you are commanded father, you will find me steadfast").

There was another myth I dreamed of, all those days as a discontented young man, not yet a poet at all, lingering by the chain-link fence clutching my copy of *D'Aulaires' Book of Greek Myths*, lingering on the story of Ganymede and imagining that of all the youths on Earth, Zeus the King of the Sky would see me and find me most beautiful, that he would soar down not in the shape of a swan or a bull or a god but as a man.

So there I was, a two-faced supplicant, the unwritten son, the one shocked between wolftongue and thunder, eternally alarmed and never ameliorated, committed beyond reason to the actual world yet all the while praying to be abducted curly-locked and fabulous into Heaven.

DRUNK TEXT

in and in between each sway
the cold is hard and solid
I wonder what is it that strays
who loves me even more

which street do I walk on now
how do I take good care
river that hid me or river that drowned
who am I now and where—

SEARCH ME

desert fell or do I find
in seven years time that famine

fine today search for dust
what finds you your disbelief

family time collecting clues
distracted by absent music

drifting across arable land
my hunger hungry to tell me

Tree Pose

Poetry lives in my body not just because there is a snake,
serpent of wisdom who spilled the beans, who slithered
into Adam's mouth and slid down his throat, already sore
from naming.

I'm lonely on the plane as it carries me away and always
wonder how far there is left to fall.

Out of the mortal shape for one thing and into the earth.

I can't answer you except to say the energy of poetry is
already coiled in my pelvis, taking up the space usually
filled by gender, that slippery genre of the body that
refuses to behave.

It's raining hard and I've one more errand to run before
hurrying home to comfort a friend and prepare for the talk
on my trip to Palestine.

I had no time this morning because I had to watch
Matthaus cutting down the tree so he wouldn't hurt
himself.

He had to take down the tree because a branch broken in the storm splintered and fell the next day and nearly hit Ella in her driveway.

Our bodies are so lovely and breakable so what does it say that they are the vessel for poetry.

Do they fill like a river or shine some light on frailty. How quickly we don't have ourselves anymore.

The rain is cold and we are water.

Matthaus came inside after his labor and marveled at the woodwork inside. The house is like a body and we are the poetry whispered inside.

Sound, music, window and sun.

The shady room on the third floor, for example, where we practice meditation and yoga. Now that the tree is gone, even in the summers it will be flooded with light.

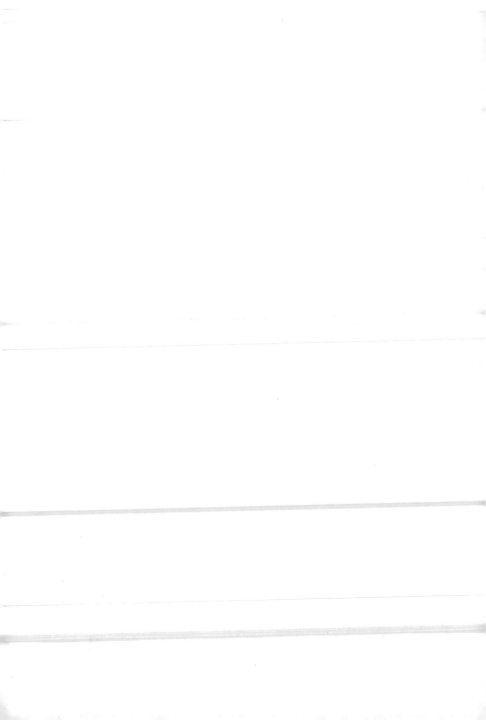

Marco and I come south to Patagonia. Here the sky looks different—the southern sky, so different from the constellations I studied when I was a boy in the far Canadian north. The only shape in the sky I recognize is Orion, but here on the other side of planet, of course, he is hanging upside down.

It's cold, cold like when we were in Uttarkhand, though that was winter in the tropics and here it is the height of summer. When the sun comes out it warms us. We took two short hikes today, one to the waterfall and another one to the Eagle's View which looks out over the whole valley, all the way to where mountains close and the river flows in.

The town is nestled against hills and ringed by the jagged and grey-white peaks. There are horses and cows wandering in the scrubby taiga meadows. The only trees are pines, and one kind—I do not know its name. We came to this small town—people come to this small town—because here the glaciers surge down out of the mountains; they cross the border from Chile down into the lakes of Argentina.

They are ancient rivers and still flowing, though infinitely slowly, transitioning throughout their journey from liquid to ice to liquid again, rolling down with the same deliberate and thunderous force that plates of continents roll together.

The ablation area is called the "tongue," and it is with that silver tongue the glacier speaks. Every once in while there is a thunderous sound—a crack from the blue heart where the glacier is melting, re-freezing, cloud, sky, mountain, and river.

This ice—solid-seeming always but in fact always in process—is nearly human.

MY LETTER TO THE WORLD IS A BODY
BUT WHAT IS IT MADE OF AND
HOW DOES IT SOUND

WHEN YOU WROTE A LETTER—WRITTEN OUT BY HAND—you pressed your pen into the page, you hoped some energy somehow traveled in. You folded the paper, you put it in an envelope, and you sealed the envelope. You stamped and sent it. And who knows who will respond.

In Urdu, time is weirdly ambiguous and flexible: the word for "yesterday" and the word for "tomorrow" is the same word—*kal*—and the listener only knows which you mean by the accompanying verb tense; also one would say "the other day" meaning anything from "the day before yesterday" to "last year." So how do you know who you are in a world of instantaneity? Now you write a letter and if you *don't* hear at once or within minutes or an hour, that silence freights itself with all kinds of meaning.

Sometimes I pick up a book of poems and read something that feels immediate, like I am being spoken to directly, in the same room even. I remain sure somehow—irrationally but firmly sure—that Olga Broumas and T Begley were writing about *me* in the following verse from their book *Sappho's Gymnasium,* though they knew nothing of me; I wouldn't meet Broumas until the fall of 2001, nearly eight years after the book was published:

> Justice missed hyperventilates poet
> Buddha vowel in Mohammed child dared cross
> far from mother olivegroves father almonds
> lyric sap of maple far from Lesvos

I had a similar feeling when in St. Mark's Bookshop—my church and my gymnasium for all the years I lived in New York City, but gone now, it doesn't exist anymore—when I picked up a little pink and orange chapbook called *New Waves* by Ben Fama. It was full of poems so ordinary but alarming. Reminded of Michael Burkard, Jean Valentine, or Fanny Howe, I read this:

> Reach into the cloud
> architecture, almost to the stars.
> I lived where they are made

The reason these poems read me so deeply is that they live in the world; they wonder, they are confused. And when they wonder they wonder with wonder:

Today I would only
take advice from an angel.
She says soon you will grow
into a beautiful girl.
Soon you will become a planet,
moons and everything.
Sometimes I feel so happy
I forget I'm going to die...

Remembering that book I read some years ago, I wrote to
Ben Fama about my cold childhood. I said, "It's cold here you
know. With piles of snow on the ground like I remember from
my cold childhood in the Canadian north. There would be so
much snow on the ground by Halloween that we would have
to shovel before going out. Of course it was a small trailer-park
town with dirt roads and no sidewalks. How did we survive
the long winters? It was full dark at 4:30 P.M., we'd all trudge
home from school in the bluing dark, snow up to our knees.
The school in town went only up to 8th grade so the older kids
went to boarding school in Wabowden, eighty-eight kilome-
ters away—".

There was so much more to tell him but even as I wrote it
down it felt like a story someone else was telling: my father an
engineer for a hydroelectric project that would dam the river
to the chagrin and economic dismay of the local Pimicikamak
people; my family the only non-natives/non-whites in the town

of four or five hundred people. None of this feels real when I explain it to other people, and the town itself, Jenpeg, Manitoba, doesn't exist anymore except as a Facebook group for people who used to live there.

But that is where I discovered the sky. More than five hundred kilometers north of Winnipeg. Lost amid the hundred-foot-tall pines, enveloped in the Canadian boreal forest with no other town anywhere nearby, at night the place was pitch dark and you could see every constellation perfectly: the Milky Way in a bolt of white silk across the apex of the sky, the occasional shimmer of Aurora Borealis along the rim of the northern horizon. My father started me from the beginning, with a good telescope and blank star charts. I learned by reading the star charts from the Winnipeg newspapers and then we would look at the sky at night and plot out the stars as they appeared to us. With some luck and my dad's stellar math skills we would aim the telescope in a different direction: Jupiter, the moons of Saturn, Arcturus, the belt of Orion; we had a different quarry each night. If there was a particularly interesting phenomenon or confluence, then the neighbors would come over, some with their own telescopes, and we would all gaze skyward.

Now some theoretical physicists are positing that everything in the universe may be a simulation, programmed by some intelligence, not even real. The idea sounds hyper-modern, like a real-life version of *The Matrix,* but something like this was spelled out in the Vedas thousands of years ago, and in more or less the same terms that the physicists are using now. You would wonder about the same thing had you had a chance to stare deep into the dark of Nothing and see what I saw those cold evenings thirty-some years ago.

In *Moby-Dick*, the little cabin boy Pip understands God when he spends a day and a night looking out at the infinity of the horizon, wondering when the ship would notice him missing and come back to fetch him. It's what Emily Dickinson saw too perhaps, that gorgeous nothing. First she wrote a letter to Thomas Wentworth Higginson, praying for what, who knows; leaving it unsigned but including a card with her signature sealed into a second smaller envelope. You must open me, she thought at him. Then she wrote poems on the insides of envelopes. Now Marta Werner and Jen Bervin have collected all the writing Dickinson did on those envelopes, arguing not necessarily that she chose the form, but that she did adapt her text to the shapes and textures of those household scraps.

Like physicists, Dickinson obsessed about time and eternity. On one ragged triangular scrap, at its delta limned by glue, she wrote, "In this short life / that only lasts an hour / merely / How much—how / little—is / within our / power." Elsewhere she wrote, "Eternity will / be / Velocity," which to me is reminiscent of the way the light and matter of stars traverse the universe, or the way sound vibration travels from source to ear.

All matter is the vibration of infinite particles, after all: Vibration—meaning sound.

In ancient yogic teachings, the ones that tell about the nature of the physical universe as a manifestation of consciousness, it is *sound* that is said to be that actual manifestation. In the mystical traditions of South Asia—both in Hinduism and Islam—music is used as a form of worship, a way of understanding the abstraction of "god" in real present terms. And with sound as its spirit, an instrument becomes a body. The yogi settles into a posture and breathes deeply to channel the energetic flow of all matter. A musician uses an actual instrument to channel breath.

I think this is why I found such great tragedy in one particular event of recent history. While a Canadian musician was traveling back through JFK airport from a tour in Morocco, the TSA confiscated and destroyed his set of bamboo *ney* flutes. The TSA asserted that the bamboo from which the flutes were made is considered agricultural contraband, and that they weren't informed of their value, along with other explanations and justifications: security risk, prohibited material, so on. The instruments were handmade by the musician himself, each of the thirteen with a different key and tone, each one's delicate body seasoned by years of playing.

The security needs of the State, its laws and regulations, work against the creation of sacred sound from the instruments of one individual.

Breath moves through the flute of the world. We imitate this when playing the instruments fashioned by our own hands.

Far away in the north country, and years and years ago, my mother and father, planet makers in the snow, mail-ordered polystyrene balls of varying sizes. With colored markers they designed each surface, one blue-green for Venus, another with the outlines of the continents for Earth, another milky-red for Mars, another with stripes and a red storm for Jupiter. My mother somehow fashioned rings for Saturn with thin cardboard cut from an oatmeal box, and then each of the nine planets were pierced with twine and hung from the ceiling of my room around the central light fixture.

Around such a sun those fashioned planets spin eternal while I the littlest astronomer sought to see—

ALL WAYS TO KNOW

it is always to change direction always to know

that I quote the sutra-soft orange threads

tying themselves in strings around the cage bars

my bony torso slick with gold squares pressed there

at Sarnath I first heard the syllables of lack

I am 'was'

I was 'want'

want that I lay myself down

smooth on a prayerboard carried forward

the window was broken

the papers were stolen

and I was no where but empty

driven to think myself endlessly forward

at Sarnath a monk tied the string around my wrist

meant to remind me but remind me of what

STAR SAILOR

courage of contrail writing peace in the sky
all my enemies retreat underground

if atlas stumbled and the sky-bell slipped
all the darkness would fall down

we would find ourselves each
stars in space

the whole world blue
and terrified

everyday Cosmonaut
I was so called

Kazim knot
what you told me

not what I claimed
not what stayed with me

naut what I was named

The Text Lover

In the hotel room I lay down next to my friend, watching him
read my poems.

He reads and I stroke his hair.

The previous night a plane had crashed in my old
neighborhood just one street over from my parents' house.

My father—his TV turned up all the way watching golden age
Bollywood movies—had heard nothing of the disaster, and
I'm on the other side of the world, having seen the news on a
television in the hotel lobby, calling, calling, frantic.

My life walking down the jet-way thinking I should leave a
copy of the poems in the hotel room drawer.

If I disappear now, they will disappear as well.

Watching the light rise off my friend's ribcage and back as he
breathed. Everything in the world that's lost.

My friend saw those poems, read them once to himself in the
blue afternoon. But what could he possibly remember?

A line, a word, a scrap.

I'm in the air now lost not lost—

've been dangerous for a long time, partly because of who I am and who I love and what I believe but partly because of how I am seen and how my body is defined in the world—not just in my own lifetime but for a thousand years or more.

A European power elite needed to exoticize and criminalize the dark body, the Middle Eastern one, the Arab one, the Persian one, the Indian one, in order to establish justification for the political control of natural resources in the region—oil, salt, indigo.

The crusade to control spirituality was only a mask for economic and social control. Resistance to the European project takes its motivation not from this historical context but rather uses historical context as a mask for forays against Europe that do not take seriously any notion that small attacks will topple those countries. Rather, the groups use attacks to shore up their power on their own homefronts.

It is an irony because the Crusades themselves were not meant to rescue pilgrimage sites from heathen hands but as cover to further political and economic control both at home and abroad.

Further irony is pointed out by Slavoj Žižek when he notes that the one who most vehemently fights the hard-line Muslim is a right-wing Christian who probably shares most of the same beliefs—about women, about gay people, about the apocalyptic end of days, and so on. And the one who defends Muslims the most—include me in that number—is the one with whom they have, perhaps, the least in common in the way of beliefs.

And yet when people began using the hashtag #IamMuslimToo in the wake of the last presidential election, I found myself bristling. How does one become the other so easily? Isn't Islam itself a philosophy of fluidity and decentered inquiry? If one can say, "I am Muslim too," ought not one just become Muslim?

Why are we who we are and not other than that? Just because of familiarity, our family, how we were raised, the shape our child-hoods made?

In an effort to understand the mind of God, the sands of time, I read yoga philosophy; I read loop quantum gravity theory; I read poetry. Sometimes I think the three are the same. If space-time folds on itself and ends where it started then maybe the Rig-Veda was right—that the universe of existence has no source—it does not end—

Not that time spirals impossibly onward but that there is no "time": that like light, which Einstein claimed exists in the same always-present moment of the Big Bang, we are all always present in the one moment of every moment in our lives. So maybe it is impossible to change, or if you change it is only a slight shift, the smallest swerve and not a transformation after all.

TELL ME AGAIN POLAR VORTEX
HOW BODIES CHANGE INTO
OTHER BODIES

AND THESE DAYS I AM REMINDED MORE AND MORE OFTEN than usual about my childhood in Jenpeg, Manitoba. The polar vortex crashes down the latitudes to meet us.

Normally this frosty weather system circles the North Pole but because of the warming Arctic Ocean it presses southwards. I am no climatologist but I know this snowy friend is the tail end of a system-wide shift that also included Hurricane Sandy traveling west into the east coast of the United States. Systems shift and change with only a little impetus from here and there.

Several years ago, as 2012—a year that was one of many predicted apocalypses—slowly shut itself down, I had one of those painful New Year's Eve party conversations with a person who I believe thought me a real space case. The more I tried to explain my point, the crazier I sounded even to myself. But now in the cold light of day, my general argument seems to me completely rational. This is what I was trying to explain: Since we as human beings are made up of metals and minerals and the earth is made of these same materials, couldn't there be something akin to magnetism that draws us to one part of the planet or another? Could that be why some of us are drawn north or south, or to rivers, mountains, or sea? And what does it say about me that I am so attached to places where mountains fall into the ocean?

Where I live, the water of the Great Lakes crawls up into the air and hovers there all winter in a thick cloud, so I've had to learn the art of the supplement—in my case Vitamin D pills on account of the dark and snowy months of lake effect, along with Vitamin B12 on account of my veganism.

Here's the rest of my New Year's argument, the part where the other person really thought I'd gone out to lunch: If human bodies are affected by minerals in the earth, which seems reasonable, then could our current states of mental health be correlated to mining and fracking? And if the moon alters tides on the earth's surface, and our blood too is a liquid and so must similarly be affected, can some physical-truth basis for astrology be so far-fetched? I lost him there. I lost myself.

But I don't mind being lost. As Claude Monet complains in Lisel Mueller's poem, "Monet Refuses the Operation, "I will not return to a universe / of objects that don't know each other, / as if islands were not the lost children / of one great continent." And as far as "pseudoscience" goes, I want to remind you that when James Lovelock first started bandying about his so-called

32

Gaia Theory—that the planet as an entire system behaves like a single self-regulating living organism, its cooling and heating periods throughout geo-history responses to external phenomena—he too was accused of drifting far afield.

But what seems in another time to be madness is later called prophecy. In the Homeric stories, the god-cursed Cassandra of Troy tried to warn her family about the Greeks' plans while her traitorous twin brother Helenus, who perhaps did believe her, went to the Greeks and gave away the Trojans' secrets. He was believed and she was not and so he managed to save his skin. Are both prophecy and madness always tied to some kind of betrayal or border-crossing? The blind clairvoyant Tiresias's ability to prophesy was accompanied by the curse (or was it a gift?) of living seven years as a man followed by seven years as a woman, and so on through the rest of life. I have yet to see a staging of a Greek play that casts a woman in the role of Tiresias, and none of the myths depict Tiresias's life as a woman, but such an experience must have given her (and him?) even greater insight into the physical world in which she (and he) lived.

Not all bodies crossing borders are content with the limitations of language. Though in Farsi pronouns are gender neutral, in English they aren't, with the exception of the subjunctive case. You have to choose. But how do you choose a gender if you have changed from one to the other? Or if you aren't either? And what if you are all genders in turn or at once? Such are also the complaints of animals and plants and trees, none of whom are deemed in the human-centered vision to have subjectivity or agency, yet who all exhibit their own intelligences. If we are wrong about gender we might be wrong about sentience. Life is lived in the subjunctive case.

In Jorie Graham's poem "Treadmill," the path before us is ever-renewing. "It wants us to learn 'nowhere,'" writes Graham. How strange a wish, for a poem in a book called *Place*, but in the end don't all of us want to know "who are you going to be when all this clay flowing through you has / finally become / form, and you catch a glimpse of yourself at daybreak, /... what was it you were told to / accomplish"?

We are at odds, for the moment, with the limits of our planet—what it can give us in the way of resources, what we can do to it in the name of getting more resources. According to Lovelock, it's not a lose-lose situation: the organism is self-regulating so will take care of us before we can ruin it beyond repair. Thus goes his so far borne-out science. Of course, this is not a completely reassuring principle to lean back on.

So the cold weather drives us indoors to huddle together for warmth. It's *supposed to*. The difference now is that heat in the winter and the ability to stay cool in the summer are both commodified. Humans, as Paul Virilio points out in his book *The Administration of Fear*, have separated from the rhythms of seasons, of night and day, and even—through medicine and surgical interventions—somewhat from processes of age and mortality.

In the summer of 2013, I taught at a writing conference at Manhattanville College alongside 1960s anti-war activist and present-day educator Bill Ayres. While he was teaching his class on memoir, I was teaching a class on yoga, meditation, and the rhythm of breath and how these might relate to the rhythm of poetry. After several days together, I finally got up the guts to ask Bill, "Do you know about the website called Weather Underground? You put in your zip code and it tells you the temperature." He laughed. "They didn't just steal our name," he said, "they stole our logo too."

In the winter, I check Weather Underground to see the dropping or rising degrees so I know how to equip myself for my daily run.

"It is possible we should have done things differently," Ayres told me one afternoon, "but we weren't wrong about what we thought. Everything that we said was going to happen with the country politically and economically has happened."

The Weather Underground sought to change the system through radical political action. They were not successful but the system as they knew it *did* change, and we have now inherited that change.

And as a political and economic system changes, the bodies inside the system change, although we have been coded, throughout our history, by caste, by race, by class, by gender— our physical bodies assigned roles and tasks deemed somehow more fit for one or the other.

CAConrad is a writer who sees the possibilities for prophetic utterance in an individual's alienation from the larger accepted social context: "It sounds strange but being queer made creativity easier for me if only because I was shunned, forced outside the acceptable, respectable world." He goes on to embrace what he calls (Soma)tic Poetry, which he describes as "the realization of two basic ideas: (1) Everything around us has a creative viability with the potential to spur new modes of thought," and "(2) The most vital ingredient to bringing sustainable, humane changes to our world is creativity." In this way Conrad creates exercises and physical practices that utilize the poem as a form of connection or re-connection with the larger whole, not just of humanity but of the entire ecosystem.

Conrad and Ayres share a political analysis—that the system of American capitalism is mostly interested in perpetuating itself at all costs, including human costs of poverty, illiteracy, and war—but their approaches to a solution, while equally radical, are different. Ayres advocated (and still advocates) a political solution, while Conrad puts his faith in the individual's capacity for creativity and creative thinking. Both Conrad and Ayres believe that the individual must put his or her own body on the line to achieve social change.

The first place Graham uses a personal pronoun in "Treadmill" is in the twenty-eighth line: "I / entered the poem here, / on line 28, at 6:44 P.M.," which is a breathtakingly weird moment. "I had been trying to stay outside, I had not wanted to / put my feet here too, but the wind came up, a little Achilles-wind, the city itself took / time off from dying to whisper into my ear we need you,..."

The planet is changing around us, but we are not going to be able to do anything unless we know who we are, not limited and bound by the mere physical conditions of a body. In a recent interview with Katie Couric, actress Laverne Cox lamented that we fixate on the physical body when talking about questions of gender and gender transitioning: "By focusing on bodies we don't focus on the lived realities of that oppression and that discrimination."

In other words, the vortex that brings the cold had its origin in some other quality of the system.

We exist in a net of infinite relationships, what Islamic philosophy calls "kismet," which Western thinkers have generally mistranslated as "fate" when the word actually means anything but. If anything, the meaning is closer to the Vedic notion of "karma," an accumulation of cause and effect that has assembled itself over an infinite period of time to manifest in the present moment. "Predetermined" *can* mean "chosen" rather than "fated."

The vortex departs from the pole, pushed by the warming waters. It brings its cold into the country of the Great Lakes. What displaces from there shifts to some other place. Equations have not yet been written to describe the new epic that is right now by the planet being written.

And who is one body, one small boy, in the face of everything outside of it? I learned many years later, a long time after, that the hydroelectric system my father helped build on the Nelson river near the northern shores of Lake Winnipeg flooded local waterways and changed the fishing patterns of the indigenous peoples, patterns they had lived by for hundreds and maybe thousands of years.

When I was a little boy in that Canadian North I wondered, swinging on the swing set after my morning breakfast of brightly colored cereal and milk during the short, chilly northern summers, who I was, who I was supposed to be in the world. I knew I belonged to the world and not the other way around, but I didn't know what I was supposed to do next.

I wondered in the crazy or poetic way that fools have, or children, *Is my body a bowl the wind is stirring or is it me that's the spoon soaring wild up to taste the cold white blue?*

PROMISES, PROMISES

Window pane teach me to do without
tools of everywhere time

Strange cup spilled the gap of fill
no one my brethren seem

No lustful stranger disturbing my house
no odd shattered flower in bed

Speaking in long forgotten tongues
no hour unpetalling thread

MOUNTAIN TIME

the mountains came south, looking into each house as they passed

in the desert I swam myself earthward to know

cacti quivering for centuries

god of multiple tongues all sacred lick me

lick me dew wet I spell the time on every space I open

open you now open me

breath and breath hollow me out

I am the architecture of eternity

margin to margin the valley sighs mountains they range

how on earth I wonder falling fast and free

will stone time ever have enough riven eons to find me

Newport Journal

Walking down the mossy steps to the beach.

Thick green ropes of bullwhip kelp, the kind of seaweed we saw at Point Reyes once, each with its green-ghost head, piles of them everywhere and sometimes a single one calligraphed across the sand.

Swift air, water always rushing three different ways.

Newport at the edge of the continent, ocean here not receding away into depth but dropping immediately.

In Seattle, the pines were so tall, with no low branches, my mind went quickly back to Jenpeg, to my cold childhood.

As in Madison, living in water, between lakes, water on three sides.

But Seattle, unlike Newport, protected from endless horizon by the islands. Here you only look and look.

Portland on the river, driving through at night, ablaze with lights.

I thought, turning off the highway from Portland to drive to Newport, on the shore, I would be trapped in the rainy night forever.

Coming through the last stand of trees into town I was shocked to find the town, big, dirty, grittier than Beacon, plainer than Shippensburg, a fishing town without fishing anymore.

Only last week, as five different people told me on the same day, a couple had been swept from the jetty out to sea.

While I walked I thought: I love it, this, walking along the edge of the sea. The sea without end.

Everything without end. Marguerite Duras gave it to me: other languages, a softer sense, other ways of knowing through the sea.

Language without knowing, without sound, without sense. *Sans cesse.*

Now sitting in a warm restaurant, drinking spicy coconut soup and reading poetry by Larry Eigner and Jean Valentine.

Lost always in loss.

I want to look at my hands. I want to say something in the language of the ocean, the language of the rain.

Hurrying back to the hotel I forewent my chance to see the second lighthouse, the more famous one at the northern end of town.

Tonight I go to the art gallery overlooking the ocean to read poems. I drink coffee and dream about transforming.

After the reading the people are very friendly and excited but then leave one by one. I invite my co-reader to have dinner but she is meeting friends and so I am left in the middle of the parking lot, alone, cold and getting colder.

I walk a little bit down the block. There is a man coming the other way walking a little dog. There is a café down the street that serves vegetarian food and hot drinks, he says.

La mer sans cesse.

I hurry down the road. I miss my father.

Each morning in the town called El Chaltén, situated in Argentina next to the great mountain named "Fitzroy" by English explorers, Marco and I planned our hikes through the hills of Patagonia. Some days we climbed up to mountain lakes, sometimes along the ridges to the glaciers.

The mountain peaks were slender, jagged. They clawed the thin fabric of the sky. It seemed not a landscape of the actual world but one of a fantasy novel or a science fiction film. Myths could be real, I realized. Gods could walk down from those slopes.

One day we even took a bus across the yellow scrubby plain to a broad lake, then were taken on a yacht with a hundred others to the mouth of a great glacial river. The rocks were aqua blue, shining in the sun, some of them tinged sky-blue, some of them so blue they were nearly black.

The people who come and stay in this town are wanderers. One tells us how he is going on a five-day walk along the glacier and across the border into Chile.

One day, Marco is tired and wants to rest halfway up the trail, so I leave him behind and hike on to the summit with another climber, though I can't keep up with him, I fall behind and reach the summit alone. Upon my return Marco was not at the rendezvous point. Though he lay only twenty feet off the path, I did not see him. Though I called out his name once or twice, it was not loud enough for him to hear me.

I do not know why I imagined that he would have left me and gone back to town, but I reasoned that is what he must have done.

Later when we finally connected and met, he pretended for a moment not to see me. We were both irritated, tired, hungry.

But the worst part of it was he felt abandoned out in the wilderness. And I realized much later that he never would have done that to me, never would have left and come back to town unless I was back with him, safe.

You do keep track of yourself by how you interact with other people. People are relational, like the quanta I learned comprise me, the snowflakes that interlock in the sky, which form themselves into crystals to fall.

SILVER ROAD OF DEVOTION SO
SHORELY SHOWN

~

THINKING ABOUT THE LONG WINTERS OF MY CHILDHOOD in the Canadian North reminds me of how much we loved the summers, and spent every minute on the playground outside the school. For some reason we would pour sand down the slide making it more slippery and then after sliding down, rather than running around to the ladder to climb up again we would try to wriggle up the chute against gravity. The body wants what's difficult.

Maybe that's why my fellow poetry workshop classmate Jason Schneiderman and I somehow managed twice a week during graduate school to make it to the 7:30 A.M. yoga class taught at the time by a woman named Julie, a former dancer. It was harder for Jason than me; he had to catch a train from Brooklyn while I just jumped out of bed and ran across Bleecker Street.

Still, it was there in Julie's fantastic astanga class that I learned how to breathe, and not just how to breathe but how to use my breath to experience my body and the external world

47

with deeper focus and deliberation. It wasn't until I'd studied with her for nearly a year that I learned that in addition to her many years dancing, Julie Carr was also a poet and had attended the same graduate program in creative writing that Jason and I were enrolled in.

Maybe the road of devotion is all of it at once—the breath that goes in and out of the body, the white bolt of stars across the northern sky, and the actual road, the one I follow every day into and around the world.

In December of 2011, I found myself in Varkala, a town in the state of Kerala near the southern tip of India, perched on a cliff overlooking the Arabian Sea. In the morning paper I read about a woman named Saraswati who climbed the nineteen steps of the Ayappan Temple and made puja.

Ayappan is peculiar among ancient gods: he was born of two men, Shiva and Vishnu—Shiva impregnated Vishnu, who was in the form of Mohini the Enchantress and who remained Mohini to carry the child to term. Ayappan has become the patron god of a men's movement in India. Rather than having become the symbol of the fluidity of gender, he has ironically become the symbol of the ultimate masculine principle. And women are not permitted in his temples.

I had started to read the papers that morning because I was stuck on the grammar of a poem I was trying to translate, a poem by Ananda Devi. I knew that what I ought to do was press forward with the energy of the poem and not worry about the grammar. Portals of energy in a poem are like the locks between energy chakras in the body. Is that "all which remains of the island are echoing footsteps of the absent"—meaning the echoes of the steps—or is it "all that remains of the absent ones on the island are their footprints"—meaning their actual physical prints? Also *les absents* in French is clunky in English: "The absent ones." "The absent" feels collective, abstract.

I see with an empty frame. The lens of loneliness has clicked back and I feel everywhere at once, everywhere I have traveled in order to feel this weird pure loneliness, in Cassis, in Corti, in Ramallah, in Seville, in Portland: I could be anywhere.

But also not: here sings the brilliant ocean and this ocean, savage and magnificent— there isn't another like it. Each place is only itself. And one is a different self in every place.

A friend invites me to Bangalore. Should I go there or stay here in Varkala for two more weeks?

The sea is pearly white with sunlight, sparkling like the little diamonds on the surface of marble or granite. I can't bear the—what?—empty days, or can't bear the end of the empty days? When what I want is to go down to the beach or go back to my room and lie down in the darkness and be still.

I think of Saraswati's tracks up the temple stairs like the silver trickle of a snail, one of the images that appears in the Ananda Devi poems I am translating. I found her small book of poems at the bookstore in Paris but it wasn't until I arrived in Pondicherry, the French city on India's southeastern coast, that

I began reading it, and not until I arrived here on the white-waved Arabian Sea that I began seeing the poems in English. Translating is experiential.

And you have to transform to translate: *Les pas de les absents* = "The footsteps of those long since gone." The stark and slightly hollow tone of the French is not "equivalent" to the heaviness of the four long flat stresses in English as I translated it. Not equivalent but "carried over."

I sit in a café on the cliff, facing out to the endless ocean.

I would paint this place in savage wide strokes of yellow and white—the glistening water, the sky that's almost nothing, the constant breeze that blows through, a caress, a *flaque*, pooling and dissipating, veils of sand, of air and light, the mosquito nets over the beds, the pendulous banana flower that hangs next to the second-floor landing on the stone staircase that climbs up the side of the building leading to my room on the third floor, the sounds of crows manically arguing their points with the darkness.

Now I traffic in the edge of melancholy and drift from there into centuries of light. Decades of rosaries. One begins to think in the rhythm of the ocean in the little seaside town perched up on the cliff.

And why shouldn't a boy who plummeted from the sky into the ocean have the courage to hold his breath, rise again to the surface, and allow the ocean to wash him ashore?

"Burrow into the chaos that buries you," wrote Christian Wiman. For a few years after school, I lost touch with both

Julie, who moved to California to do her PhD, and Jason, who stayed behind in New York to teach when I moved up the river to Rhinebeck. Jason wrote chillingly about the body, in particular about his mother's death, in a series of poems that appear in his second book, *Striking Surface:* "She had never / been the axis my world turned on, but suddenly / everything seemed to revolve around her. No. / Not an axis. A skewer. A spit."

How brave can one be to go so deep inside, to be willing to be impaled on the pain of one's material? How else do you earn god (whatever that word may mean)?

Translating Devi's poems has been excruciating—she's plainspoken where I weave and dodge, her emotions lie close to the surface whether grief or rage, and mine, oh mine they just drift every which way, so fraught is every feeling for me. But walking deep inside her words trained me, trained me so well to "strain to hear / The voices of those absent / Until the night at last / agrees to speak to you."

Devi showed me that not only the light and pure and breath-filled but the dark and vexed and painful must also find their beauty in poetry.

On the Tamil Nadu coast just north of Pondicherry, there is a temple that was reclaimed from the ocean. The guide tells me of the legend that there were once seven temples along the shore, the other six still submerged under waters. During the 2004 tsunami, the water drew back and people could see the rubble and outlines of them, eroded but there still, exposed to air after a thousand watery years.

And in Kerala, Saraswati begins to climb the eighteen sacred steps to the Ayappan Temple.

So, having outlived Federico García Lorca at the unlit olive tree I rip fruit from each dark pit. I walk from the sea inside a mouth pronouncing echoless voices. What was the bail for the sunbird set at? How does he plead to the crime of harnessing the wind and traveling the acres of sky?

It is not enough to redraw the maps of nation or body, but one must also parcel up the streams to send to the parched valleys. The ocean's greed is endless. During the long fasting month we draw fantasies of liberation on our side of the long tough wall.

The day after she offered puja, Saraswati stands at the foot of the temple watching the priests purify the altar and re-sanctify the building.

When I open my mouth it fills with dirt.

I stand at the bottom of the temple steps, looking up at Saraswati's shining tracks, the ones leading up the temple stairs, defiling and divine.

They lead to heaven, so impurely shown.

THE SUITCASE

A crazy shape floating in from far away. Fanny said it looked like a body. Horror grew in us until we saw: a deflated balloon, silver, saying "happy birthday." Is it your birthday, I asked Fanny. "It is," she wailed, her blue eyes terrifed with delight.

Walking along the beach she told me, "This is the same beach where we found wreckage from the plane crash. The suitcase."

Years later I remembered this, standing in the cathedral square of Málaga, looking up at the unfinished south tower, climbing fiercely up from the nave and then:

Blue: like Fanny's eyes, like the canvas flowers on the suitcase, like the sky-cold ocean, no tower, no bells, just an endless ceasing, what comes floating in—

BAGGAGE CLAIM

maybe I am   a suitcase unspoken for   a seed
inside the sealed 'seem'   stitched between breath and body

me and my   dreaming mind   reaching for
the blue canvas case   conveyed out of grasp

memory of my mother   memory of   all that disappears
in the endless vision overhead   of waves

a plane crashing into water   a suitcase washed ashore
what am I made of   water   am I made of   fire

and my mother is still dreaming trying to remember
where is my claim check   what is my name

Portland Journal

Craig bends over his table of light, tracing so carefully stroke
by stroke his calligraphed patterns of *nastaliq* for another panel
of the book he is working on, a graphic novel called *Habibi*.

By the window condensed air trickling down in streams.

Cold outside but not for me, raised in the Canadian north.

Portland: named for a city in the east, another city on the
water. The last time I was here I was in the world of politics,
not poetry.

Tonight my friends from those years and years past will join
us.

To see them again will remind me of who I am now, who I
was then.

Any difference in these is the same as the difference between
the water in the ground or the water in air unraveling.

Yesterday Craig took me to his favorite bookstore, a temple
for us both, where we spent hours.

And then, drowned or high with pleasure, the most exciting part: an ordinary life: errands to pick up his jacket, to the bank, to drink coffee, to pick up ink from the art supply store.

Somewhere along our trip my bag disappeared, my new notebook inside plus my new manuscript of poetry, the one about the river cloud sutra, with all of my notes and corrections.

River cloud: the story of how the water of a river will condense into the air making a snaking cloud that runs along the length of the river.

How we all transform.

Portland: the flocks. Murder of crows perching angry on the car screaming.

My bag with its notebook of poetry and my annotated manuscript perches secret in the check-shelves at Powell's.

French for secret: caché.

The secrets I told and then the other ones, the ones I wrote on my skin in calligraphed letters, the wet ink licking me stroke by stroke.

Remind me, remind me what light comes through me, what it seizes on its journey through the window, through the table, into the lines of the calligraphed letters, line of the horizon at the shore, line of light, lying across the table, lines in my palm.

And dead this morning to suddenly realize what's missing in the world is what is part of the inside-life.

Last night there was a verse Craig drew into the surface of the water, but looking in the book it seemed one word was transcribed differently, a word we didn't know.

I wrote it in the condensed air on the pane of glass.

Am I cold inside still, wondering where my old lovers are today, wondering if my body still sings to them, wondering how poetry came out of me, wondering how I will find my way through the streets back to the bookstore to claim my secret bag, the poems and notes written inside.

Sun yellow but still cold, the dusting of snow yet unmelted.

The woman at the bookstore asks me to describe the contents of the bag and I can't because I don't remember which journal it is, and didn't write my name inside it.

In *Blankets*, the graphic novel Craig wrote about his childhood, he only wrote of two brothers; he left out his sister. What do I leave out, or is it just that there are things we haven't yet looked at, stories we are not yet ready to tell?

The leaves are nearly all fallen from the trees. Some will not fall after all but will freeze red on the branch.

n November—before we've left for South America—my sister
enters the hospital for a stem-cell transplant treatment. This has
long been used to treat leukemia patients but she is in a trial
treatment for her Multiple Sclerosis. It is possible that the new
stem cells will regenerate her immune system and halt the prog-
ress of her MS symptoms or even reverse some of the damage.

No one will be able to tell until the cells are drawn, her immune
system eradicated by chemotherapy, the cells treated and swirled
and reinserted into her.

Since I am on leave from teaching, I am the one most available to
go and stay with her in isolation, where I spend weeks scrubbing,
disinfecting, cleaning, cooking. During the days we occupy the
time by watching endless episodes of Little House on the Prairie. In
the evenings I go out and wander the streets of Chicago just to
remind myself that I am someone else besides a caregiver.

Though at the same time it feels incredible to be a caregiver, to
give my whole own identity over to someone else. And to be
someone in my family, not just the middle child, the gay son who
is assumed to not care anything about his parents' wishes, about
the culture he came from, the religion he was raised in.

The prodigal son tenderly takes his sister to have all her hair
cut off because she knows she will lose it anyhow. The son runs
interference with doctors, nurses, with well-meaning relatives

who want to visit. He thinks the sister never even knows how he shepherds people in and out, helps his mother to "decide" not to come on the days the sister is run down to the bone, how he subtly encourages another relative whom she hasn't heard from in a while to call on the day the sister is feeling especially down.

Months later he will find out that the sister knew—despite the brother's every effort—she knew all along the tricks he was playing on everyone.

She has been sick for decades. After the operations, after the weeks of chemotherapy and the convalescence, she goes home to Florida, and the brother boards a plane for Toronto—for the funeral of their Aunty Najma—and then another plane to South America—to visit his *other* family, the family of his partner, the family that no one in his first family has ever met.

So I go with Marco south to the mountains, but I keep remembering the time with my sister, how I took the phone or the remote control whenever she needed to use them and gave them each a quick spray and a swipe, the time I spent on hold with the airline changing my tickets when I learned of my aunt's passing.

And that is why and how one moves from first person to third person and back.

CLIMB UP SURE BUT DO YOU KNOW
WHERE YOU ARE GOING

‿

IN EARLY 2014, ISRAELI SETTLERS ENTERED the grounds of the Temple Mount in Jerusalem and climbed on top of the structure of the Dome of the Rock. Some years earlier, when I went to Israel, we had entered the plaza, called Al-Aqsa, the "far place," through the portals that lead up stone staircases from streets in the eastern part of the city. There were Muslim caretakers at these gates and to ensure that those entering were worshipers and not tourists nor vandals (there has been trouble in both that place and other Muslim and Christian sites—violence and vandalism), those passing through the gates are asked questions pertaining to religious knowledge, sometimes asked to recite certain verses from the Qur'an. You have to know, or you don't enter.

There is another entrance. It is a security checkpoint in the Jewish Quarter just next to the Western Wall. You go through a metal detector, your bags are searched and you pass through a little covered causeway up to the Mount. It is not unlike the gates that bring one from an airport terminal onto a plane. There, on the wide plaza, amid park-like areas and open spaces, is the Far Mosque, built in the fifteenth century or thereabouts on the site of an older mosque that had been destroyed, and the glittering Dome of the Rock. Inside that gold-domed structure is, indeed, the Rock.

It's an odd piece of real estate. I saw rocks as huge in Hyderabad, where an ancient mountain range, over the course of seventy million years, has been shattered to pieces—the destruction of that mountain range is believed by some scientists to have caused the dramatic climate change that brought about the end of the dinosaurs. But the particular rock on Al-Aqsa in Jerusalem has what could be an even more mythic history: some say this is the place Adam and Eve entered the Earth after expulsion from Eden; some say the place where Abraham took his son, Ishmael or Isaac, to be sacrificed; some say the place to which Prophet Muhammad was brought on his night journey from Mecca and from which he launched up into heaven.

And/or: it is a rock.

In any case, *no one* is allowed to climb up on top of the Rock, although—if you are Muslim, or if you know enough Qur'anic verses to recite, or accompany a friend who does—you can descend into a chamber in the heart of the rock called the "Well of Souls," the place the Ark of the Covenant is purported to have been kept.

I went down inside. What I saw there, softly illuminated, what that space was like, what I did there and how it felt, I will not say. We keep some secrets and some secrets, they keep us.

What is a nation? A place of common language, common origin, common cultural values and structure? What is it meant for? To protect you, to promote your economic or religious interests, to guarantee you access to natural resources? Empires were founded to bring from far places spices, vegetables, metals, and minerals. But really, I want to know, and this isn't a rhetorical question: Who owns a place and why?

One of my favorite scriptural stories is about the king of Babel, who decided to build a tower to reach heaven, which is only an interesting place because a god lives there. Of course, as the story goes, God cursed the builders by fracturing their language so they could no longer communicate with each other to build—the origin of poetry was the human urge to actually reach the geography of the divine. What are the implications of such thinking? Was poetry a curse or a gift? A response to the urge to build an edifice to reach what they thought was the actual physical place God lived, but which we know now is nothing but air?

Perhaps the story appeals to me because to me the most meaningful structures of worship are ones that are incomplete.

The set-up for visitors and worshipers in the small plaza in front of the accessible fragment of the Western Wall seems completely impromptu—there were plastic lawn chairs pulled up next to it, so people could sit and pray. Considering the diasporic nature of the Jewish people, the tenuous nature of any of their claims to "home" throughout their long history, this felt oddly appropriate. And on the causeway leading up to the Mount, very neatly stacked—for quick and easy access one supposes—we saw scores and scores of riot shields. Chairs and shields, the two stackable objects told a stark story. And anyhow, as my friend who lives in Israel, a religious Jew, tells me, one of the names for God in Hebrew is "the Place," so why do we end up taking *any* place on Earth as sacred? There is no road to heaven. Ask Saraswati, the woman accused of defiling the Ayappan Temple by praying there as a female. Ask the builders of Babel.

The divine must live in the mortal world, then. In her poem "After a Student, 15, Declares He Will Renounce the World for God," Kathleen Graber has the forsythia bush speak: "I'm forever. I'm all the evidence you need." And of the tower of Babel, she dreams of being one of the builders, thinking, "how the gods must stop here / at their own reflections." All we have at the end is our "beautiful confusion."

Living in the world, embracing that confusion, means using the body to understand the spirit. In her poem "Love Isn't," Pat Parker confesses, "I wish I could be / the lover you want / come joyful / bear brightness / like summer sun // Instead / I come cloudy / bring pregnant women / with no money / bring angry comrades / with no shelter." There is no separation in Parker's reality between caring for the individual and being concerned with larger issues of social justice. "I care for you," she says to her lover, "I care for our world / if I stop/ caring about one / it would be only / a matter of time / before I stop / loving / the other."

Parker's insistence on the inseparability of both concerns may feel anachronistic in our time. Consider Amiri Baraka's pointed criticism of *Angles of Ascent*, the recent Norton anthology whose jacket claims of its contents, "These poets bear witness to the interior landscape of their own individual selves or examine the private or personal worlds of invented personae and, therefore, of human beings living in our modern and postmodern worlds." Baraka called that view "embarrassing gobbledygook" and "imbecilic garbage," saying, "You mean, forget the actual world, have nothing to do with the real world and real people...invent it all!"

Parker views such a practice—the examining of an interior landscape *without* also engaging in historical and material context—to be a form of insanity. In the foreword to her powerful book *Jonestown and Other Madness*, Parker writes, "I must ask the question: if 900 white people had gone to a country with a Black minister and 'committed suicide' would we have accepted the answers we were given so easily?" She creates a critical confluence between our ability to either engage or disengage from issues of social injustice and the bodies that are victims of such injustice. The people who went to Jonestown and drank the cyanide-laced juice and died there—nine hundred and eighteen in all, most of them Black, most of them women—seem thereby to be irrelevant, less worthy of concern.

Discussing the origins of her poem "Power," Audre Lorde talks about anger at injustice as a genesis for creative expression: "A kind of fury rose up in me; the sky turned red. I felt so sick. I felt as if I would drive this car into a wall, into the next person I saw. So I pulled over. I took out my journal just to air some of my fury, to get it out of my fingertips."

In Nevada in 1980, there was a case of a woman who, rather than find expression, succumbed to such anger. Priscilla Ford drove her car off the road into a crowd, injuring twenty-three people and killing six. Though expert witnesses testified that she was suffering from a variety of mental illnesses, the judge and jury believed her competent and able to tell right from wrong, and they sentenced her to death. Parker writes of her in a poem called "one thanksgiving day": "You cannot be insane / to be enraged is not insane / to be filled with hatred is not insane /.../ it is your place in life" and went one to say, "The state of Nevada / has judged // that it is / not crazy / for Black folks / to kill white folks / with their cars."

Baraka famously asked for "poems that kill," by which I believe he meant poems that could confront boldly the real lived conditions of people's lives. I found such poems in the work of Lucille Clifton, who did not in any way shy away from embracing a Black aesthetic and went so far as to say, "white ways / are the ways of death..." In her poem "the thirty-eighth year," she refers to her own death as "the final europe." In the following short poem about Little Richard, she similarly uses

the word "faggot" ironically while defending Little Richard's
sexuality and non-conforming gender expressions:

> richard penniman
> when his mama and daddy died
> put on an apron and long pants
> and raised up twelve brothers and sisters
> when a whitey asked one of his brothers one time
> is little richard a man (or what?)
> he replied in perfect understanding
> you bet your faggot ass
> he is
> you bet your dying ass

For me the beginning of nations—the beginning of our sep-
aration from one another, the beginning of the rules of gender
and sexuality that would come to govern how wealth was trans-
ferred from one generation to another through stuctures of in-
heritance—is antithetical to the life of the individual human life
and spirit. And me? My sacred place is no Rock, no remnant of a
wall of a temple that hasn't existed for a thousand years. Rather
it is my favorite kind of church—the wide open and interactive
space of any museum where paintings hang or any place poetry
is recited or dance is performed.

Last year I climbed up into the "Tower," an exhibit space
in the National Gallery of Art, to see the series of paintings by

Barnett Newman called "The Stations of the Cross." Newman himself used to talk about the place a painting is hung as a "makom," Hebrew for "place," with all the connotations of sacred. Harry Cooper, the curator of the show, wrote, "the Stations might seem to raise the question 'Where am I?' Is my proper place in front of each of the paintings, one by one, or walking by them, or turning around in the middle of the room to try to take in the series as a whole? For that matter, am I in an art gallery at all or, as the title suggests, passing the Stations on the road to Calvary?"

There's no answer to the question. I went along the Via Dolorosa myself when I was in Jerusalem, or as much of it as I could. The first station is inside a private building. The last is inside a church, of course. But somewhere north of the walled city in East Jerusalem, in a park very near to where all the taxis to Ramallah wait for their passengers, there is a smaller garden which others claim is the "real" site of Calvary. Who can say?

It makes no difference to me. Mosques are empty inside, being just four walls that organize a space in which worshipers gather. There's no *there* there. Olga Broumas writes about this in her poem "Diagram of an Abandoned Mosque":

1 The loggia circled by mouths of sleep
2 We startle leaving the garden
3 Medallions of traffic and steel
4 But phantoms

5 Of circulars evolved by blood
6 Ripple orgasmically still as though power
7 And architecture were not one

But power and architecture *are* one, after all. The architecture of a building and the engines of financial, political, and military control are not unrelated. Of the men and women who went to Jonestown, Pat Parker says, "they didn't die at Jonestown / they went to Jonestown dead / convinced that America / and Americans / didn't care."

"On a day when i would have believed / anything," writes Lucille Clifton, in her own poem about Jonestown, "i believed that this white man...was possibly who he insisted he was."

Newman gave his "Stations of the Cross" paintings a subtitle: "Lema Sabachthani"—"Why did you forsake me?"—the cry Jesus launched up at God as he died.

And what are the stakes then? "If i have been wrong, again," Clifton's speaker at Jonestown goes on to say, "may even this cup in my hand turn against me."

"This is the Passion," Newman said. "Not the terrible walk up the Via Dolorosa, but the question that has no answer."

DOME OF THE ROCK

It's never been there
What you believe

Ocean or mountain
Who could choose

What heaven clamors for
No one counts on

Three times zero is
The old way home

A CARTOGRAPHY

Sketching the outlines of something
Knowing by heart how far one travels
How far did I travel to Haifa or the sea
With Rachel in the mountains
How could we have known how long history would echo

For example the mosque on the road
We didn't know if it was destroyed in a war or by neglect
One side leaning dangerously down
Inside covered with graffiti in four languages
The mihrab blackened by fire

No less holy since its primary purpose is to mark direction
In an otherwise empty building
One corner of the room completely exposed to the fields
And across the street a dead animal lying on its side
Three ropes hang down from the minaret

Where some Hasidic boys had scaled the side
And sat on the balcony—what were they doing?
Eating sandwiches, saying their prayers or listening
To the language of the land, the abandoned building or
The carcass lying limp on the side of the road

Laramie Journal

Rocks bright yellow, thirty feet high and we walk small
between them.

Sapphire sky and glowing white on the ground, rock-bones,
rock-bed, rock-wonder.

I climb frightful inside the house of stone and spell myself.

In fragmented space and time one sees oneself in slivers and
snatches.

Labors of Psyche in ordinary time I climb up on the rock-trails
but wanting only the flat ground, the field.

Field of snow, sanctified Matthew, Shepard of everybody.

Every body lashed to the fence, latched to spirit slowly
draining from the body in two clear tracks.

What I said to the Missouri students about "mountain time":
that mountains in fact mark time.

Clattering in my mind as the snow comes down, I lose
myself, lose everything.

Matthias and Julia come, and Eula and Anna, I don't feel alone for the moment.

November in the ground in Laramie snow.

Small book of sentences and theory is bliss because it is the mind wondering about the word or world behind the world or word.

Half of anything (but loneliness) and you are in negative quantity and left.

Left with nothing, all these years and death between us, Janis Joplin still wailing away on the radio.

Why so haunted by ghosts or ghosts of an idea.

Because half loneliness and you are still left there with half and besides lonely for your loneliness.

We trudge through November snow to reach actually nowhere.

Fence gone and emptiness gone: housing developments on two sides and a superstore and parking lot on the third.

Fourth stretches away and away into half loneliness, disappeared death.

Actually nowhere marked.

Take it, take another little piece of my heart.

n Buenos Aires, before we came to El Chaltén, we saw a
museum exhibit, Brazilian modernist artists. There was a painting
by Roberto Matta that I loved, and it reminded me that I
have seen his paintings many times before, the last time in San
Francisco, I believe.

There was also a series of drawings that were sketches for the
sets of a play. Interspersed in these were studies for the sketch-
es—just the shapes and instructions written on the side of the
pages. It occurred to me that a poem is like that, a sketch or
design in metaphor for something not actually built.

And you make a whole series of sketches because it is you con-
tinuing to try.

For example me, each time I try to move away from the same old
vocabulary, the same kinds of insights.

Why am I a poet at all? I never know how to answer. Because I
want to venture into the unsung, the dizzy, the dark, to know what
there might be to know.

I turned from the sketches and there was a drawing in blue ink
with a little gold of a constellation that was perhaps Draco or
maybe not. I love the sky in the south because all the patterns are
new, all the stories about them unfamiliar.

And that too seems a good metaphor: the poem is not a thing itself. We drew these lines to make a shape, but the stars themselves are organized by the eye and the narrative and the false notion of proximity, shape, and "thing-ness" only from our perspective in the galaxy. The same stars would be unrecognizable seen from a different point, or may not even exist in the same frame.

THERE ARE CRYSTALS IN STONE AND PRESSURE IN SNOW SO ARE SNOW AND STONE THE SAME

∽

As snow falls again thickly out the window I am wondered twice. First that it is a wonder at all that it snows in the winter again, so quickly and fully have I adjusted to the new reality of climate change, and the warm winters it seems to have been bringing over the past many years.

But second that snow is a *system*. Like the streaks of *Matrix* code running vertically down Mouse's screen, inside snow—its physical structure, its chemical makeup, its origins in metamorphosis, its passage from water in the sky to a crystalline thing falling to the ground—is the story of all stellar creation.

You might have to love that. At any rate, the sight of snow falling always puts me in mind of one of my favorite days—in kindergarten, in Jenpeg, being given a little blue square of felt by the teacher as we all dressed again in our snowsuits and moonboots, donned scarves, gloves, and hats and trooped outside into the recess field, where Remembrance Day ceremonies and town gatherings were also held. As the snow fell thickly we held our blue squares aloft to catch a flake or two, or three. Suspended there, caught in the thick felt weave we could—if we were careful and did not breathe directly on them—observe the full crystal structure of the flakes.

And so I grew up to be a poet and a thinker about poetry.

The body is a system, too, of course. All my glorious yoga teachers—is it coincidence that besides Julie, two others of them are also writers?—have been teaching me that, by using joints and sinews and breath. Take one of my favorite poses—*supta virasana,* or "reclining hero's pose." From a hands and knees position, draw the knees to touch and separate the lower legs, as you turn the tops of the feet flat on the ground and point them straight back. With the hands, roll the calves out and then lower the pelvis down in the space between the feet.

It's hard to do. You might have to put a cushion or padding between the feet and sit on that. There are three things happening at once: 1) the quadriceps are stretched long (keep those knees together); 2) the front of the ankle stretches (keep the toes pointing straight back); 3) the lower back and core are strengthened. Pull the stomach in and upward and sit up tall, broadening both the collar bone area and the upper back at once.

What I love is how—as B. K. S. Iyengar used to say—an asana happens in the whole body at once. There's no part of the body that isn't involved, even if it is in release, and often several oppositional movements are happening simultaneously.

And now lie back, bringing the upper back to the ground and stretching the arms over the head. I'm in heaven now just writing about it. "Earth will not let go our foot / except in her sea cup she lets us float," writes May Swenson, and I feel just as held in a yoga asana; the harder it is, the better. The practice of yoga, like the writing of a poem, is a necessary movement deeper into the difficult regions of the physical. In fact, it is a traveling up to the nation of failure and dwelling there.

Even better, my teacher Sondra once told me, is when you come face to face with your ego in a difficult posture: "Why aren't I good enough to write this poem? Why aren't I strong enough to balance in this pose?" Dwell in the failure and feel the sense of separation evaporate. "Burning up the ego in the fire of the Self," Sondra called it. Swenson believed this, too. Her poems are so intensely physical in their subjects and the language, as if the poetic line were itself body trying to breathe itself into a further contortion.

Here she is in a poem called "MAsterMANANiMAl":

> ANiMAte MANANiMAl MAttress of Nerves
> MANipulAtor Motor ANd Motive MAker
> MAMMAliAN MAtrix MAt of rivers red
> MortAl MANic Morsel Mover shAker

Language is snow in sky falling down, language is a geography itself, and Swenson knows: geography is no permanence but a shifting metamorphosis of stone, itself as exactly crystal-line and tender as snow but with a much longer timeline for the change. Snow evaporates instantly under breath and stone will do so just as thoroughly but in an "instant" whose relationship to our own perceptual capabilities is radically different.

That might be one reason I find myself first in New York then in Jerusalem, dizzy with altitude sickness while driving out of the mountains from Laramie to Boulder, or leaving the plains of Dehra Dun for the precariously teetering car journey up into the Himalayan foothills.

I can't see unless I see differently. A curse or a gift, no one can say. Likely both.

There's a whole genre of poets who seem to agree, and we follow Basho, travelling his "narrow road" to the North. And why do we leave our homes so quickly, and even in our own homes prefer to seek experiences outside the realm of our own bodies? Steve Abbott, in his book riffing on Basho that is called *Skinny Trip to a Far Place*, writes on Day Ten of that poetic diary:

> The train starts outside my window at five a.m. It's probably the beginning of a solipsistic novel, but no, it's just another haiku:

> Traffic below on Sanjo-dori
> waves of memory—like vacuum
> cleaner sound when I was 3.

To think, took ten days to notice. But it's starting to
rain and the poem says nothing of this.

Abbott notices here, not just that even when one is paying
attention one isn't paying attention, but also that the poem in
its traditional lyric form cannot hope to encompass the myriad
directions of attention of a life when it is actually *lived*.

After all, as Salman Rushdie has observed, the seemingly
reactionary ending that Hollywood tacked on to their film ad-
aptation of the Populist-inflected book *Wizard of Oz* might read
"There's no place like home" for comfortable mainstream het-
eronormative individual bodies, but for everyone else it might
better be put, "There's no place *that's* home."

Rather than a "sequence" of poems that progress from one
to another, Basho's diary is—like the projects that have descend-
ed from it, including Abbott's *Skinny Trip to a Far Place*—multi-
valent, poly-vocal, multi-genre, but most of all *quotidian*, which
means: 1) concerning itself not with high moments but with
ordinary life as it happens, and, perhaps more importantly, 2)
with a structure that unfolds day by day, returning to themes
every once in a while or perhaps bringing something up only
once and dropping it, never to be heard from again.

We may have needed Basho to give this form to us, but sev-
en hundred years earlier, give or take, women in Japan actually
invented interactive quotidian literature in the form of daytime
soap opera (Murasaki Shikibu) and blog (Sei Shonagon) and

serialized fantasy epic (*The Tale of the Heike*). Before there was *Game of Thrones* there was the Imperial Palace of the Suzaku Emperor. You think Cersei Lannister is evil? You need to meet the Rokujo Lady. She'll kill you in your dreams without even breaking a sweat.

When I was in the ancient stone city of Mahabalipuram, some hours south of Chennai along the Tamil coast, I saw not only the Shore Temple—whose six thought-to-be-mythical sister temples were revealed to be real when the tsunami of 2004 caused the ocean to recede, revealing the rubble and ruins of these temples, submerged for more than a thousand years—but countless other temples, carved into the monstrous boulders scattered around the town.

Just behind the magnificent façade of "Arjuna's Penance," carved in stone at the center of town, I found a small complex of temples whose primary design motif was a pattern of double helices. Of course I immediately started concocting science fiction about how the ancient Gupta sculptors came to understand DNA as the building block of human life. Speculation aside, the spiral does represent how a human perceives time and space—a little bit at a time, always doubling back then moving forward, living in the past and the future and the present at once.

In the physiology of yoga these spirals exist in the human body's energetic network as well—in postures we sometimes imitate this spiraling action. In the seated spinal twist, one must ground one sitting bone firmly to the ground at the same time as turning the upper body in the other direction. The spine twists and we breathe deeply, sitting up tall and grounding down, living at once in both realities.

THEFT

Bicycle missing from the shed in the night
On the screen porch no wind moves through

The cat wants to chew through the string
Tied on my wrist meant to remind me

Maybe the bicycle was not stolen but ridden and forgotten
Oh the thief of strings creeps orange through the night

Whispering his hot breath wet in my ear
Nibbling away at what holds me

MY CHEWED BOOK

After forty days god blows a spirit into the clot says the Qur'an
And after forty more days it comes to look like a chewed morsel

There is an Antarctic opening in the spine of the sky
I have no ambition for the structure of sign any more

Dream got traced on leaves tied to the sky
I'm tied forward to launch

A baby plucked a book from my hand once
And put it spine first in his mouth to chew

Boulder Journal

Traveling down two thousand feet or more, Laramie to Boulder, from the mountains to the mountains.

Mountains that themselves were thrust up from the ocean floor.

We are each one another and an other another, seen and scene seen.

Afraid of the air that thins and I reach to breathe.

Bhanu Kapil on the phone gives me directions, explains how to find things; it feels like a map in breath and air and I take it and I wander.

Silence turning forty.

Was I a refugee when I climbed into the cave outside Laramie, wishing only to transform.

I was gleeful to be there, to have finally found it, past the great bone thrust in the earth, marking not death but eternity.

Beth told me about the town around the tragedy, who were the people who were left after the story was told.

I had found Laramie a strange place but not as cold as I expected. In Peter's house there was a big church-choir chair that used to belong to Craig Arnold. I met him once, only a month before he disappeared while hiking a volcano.

Craig had *eros* tattooed on one arm and *psyche* on the other.

Aspens along the trail groaning in the wind.

On the trail, snow in our hair. The others wanted to turn back but I wanted to go on.

Bhanu sends her friend Jarvis, a maker of maps, to pick me up from my hotel to walk over to the small Naropa campus.

Strangely I am reminded of a military installation. The sycamore under which Allen Ginsberg taught; the courtyard above which the Flat Irons loom.

Says Bhanu: the campus was placed here because Chogyam Trungpa wanted the mountains to reflect back to us everything about our selves we cannot bear to face.

What is it I cannot bear to face?

At the hotel on a television talk show the woman asks, "What is the one thing you hate about yourself?"

And I feel immediately dizzy because I had so many different answers: my body, my mind, my smile, my mouth.

I could go on.

Mapped my way to myself, mapped my body and its weaknesses. Mapped the city up and down, by walking and then by driving. Every plane and hotel room the same but perhaps for one small element or another.

A city moves through time. George Perec disproved this, though, in *An Attempt at Exhausting a Place in Paris*, where he shows that cities are immediate, floating on top of the table of history as it moves.

A map has a somatic quality—ways of performing a map or performing a book.

A start of a reading list for a course on cities:
Paris France, Gertrude Stein
Of Cities and Women: Letters to Fawaz, Etel Adnan
Paper City, Nathalie Stephens
My own *Bright Felon: Autobiography and Cities*
An Attempt at Exhausting a Place in Paris, George Perec

Later Bhanu came and I had a headache and so we went to the oxygen bar and the man put tubes in our nostrils and turned the tanks on. Bhanu blissed out, leaning back against the sofa while I got hyper alert, my lungs and torso and stomach and abdomen filling, filling, filling with breath.

I asked her if she really truly did throw her manuscript in the garden to compost over the winter as she claimed she had. She said she did. She gave the composted book to Jarvis, who made a map of it.

Everywhere I walked with Jarvis I tried to take photographs of the mountains looming overhead to show this little town at the foot of the Rockies.

At the end of my visit Jarvis gave me the object he made of Bhanu's muddy decomposed pages.

But some things do not translate, some places cannot be mapped.

lived in Jenpeg, Manitoba, in the last half of the seventies. I was only a child but it was there I saw the sky, there in a town not on any maps, a town that doesn't exist anymore, there where I discovered time.

How to explain what it meant to be in the arms of the forest, in the arms of wild sounds and dark winters. As I struggle to think through all of this, I write an e-mail to the Chief of the Pimicika-mak Nation, the name of the indigenous people of Cross Lake. I speak with David, the councillor in charge of forestry and water and the agreement made with Manitoba Hydro. I tell him I want to know what happened in Jenpeg.

The dam my father helped to design and build brought hydro-electric power to the entire province. But what happened to the trees, the rivers, the lakes in that region? What happened to the fish and wildlife? And what happened to the people?

David tells me that he will show me. That I should come. He invites me to participate in a sweat lodge ceremony, and he says they want me to participate so that I can approach the land with some small understanding of their relationship to it.

I have sought ways forward through yoga, through physics, through philosophy and poetry and the body. But, despite the fact that my own partner is a gardener and a farmer and a lover of wild things, I had never really sought my way forward through the land.

But perhaps it is by going *back*, back into my own history, that I might learn. For years I lived among a people I never knew. For years I lived in a place in the world that I did not understand.

THERE ARE MORE CELLS IN ONE HUMAN BODY THAN THERE ARE STARS IN THE UNIVERSE

⤴

THE BODY IS A WAY OF UNDERSTANDING THE UNIVERSE and so the universe must be a way of understanding the body. The deepest thinking that one does about either is less as a scientist and more as a poet. The intuitive leaps that quantum and particle physics make about the nature of reality are akin to the leaps made in poetry.

This is why, as is true in Douglas Adams's book *The Hitchhiker's Guide to the Galaxy*, that "42" may be as good an answer as any to life, the universe, and everything. And yet, as the punch line goes, what is the question? In the ancient epic of the *Ramayana*, Hanuman takes a leap from the mainland of India to the island of Sri Lanka. It's a fantastic story and there is a fantastically difficult yoga asana named after the feat. But what's better is that now, using space-imaging satellites, a real bridge, seemingly human-made by its structure of regularly placed limestone boulders, has been revealed to be stretching across the ocean from the mainland to the island.

As Donald Revell writes, "The moon is hawk of the waste spaces... / / I had a good day and then another / I was married to mountains on all sides of me."

I know there's a system—obvious in every breath—that binds together all matter, inanimate and animate. In Western thought, there is a scientific principle that matter neither appears nor disappears but is constant; and if matter is constant in time, so I figure, then it must be constant in space, meaning it is the *same* matter. In Eastern thought, a principle governs the energy of action: the law of *karma*, which says that all motion affects all other motion; that the universe is a set of *relationships*, sometimes called "the diamond net of Indhra"; that all events in your own life are seeds of future karma, meaning they will manifest in some way; and that all events in your own life are manifestations of *past* karma. Wrap your head around these ideas for a minute.

In Islamic philosophy, one does not believe in "fate"—pre-ordination, predestination—but rather *kismet*, which is closer to the notion of karma, because it incorporates matter and energy and *human will* into a single gesture. Kismet includes *all* actions, there being no such things as a "success" or a "failure" as they are traditionally conceived of. Think of a series of events that ripples rhizomatically, multi-directionally, and goes beyond the body, beyond the purely physical universe and into a space of intention and attention. At the minutely small level, atoms and quanta of energy travel multi-directionally; they exist not as static points but as particles in relationship to one another. The heat and vibrations they make as they interact create the physical universe.

To me the poem is what we can make of language and breath to travel into this space.

Jack Halberstam invokes failure differently as well: as one locus where the queer body can make its stand against the heteronormative injunction to conform. In *The Queer Art of Failure*, Halberstam writes that fellow theorist José Esteban Munoz "explains the connection between queers and failure in terms of a utopian 'rejection of pragmatism,' on the one hand, and an equally utopian refusal of social norms on the other." The physical universe does not operate pragmatically, in fact. The universe is indeterminate—there are any number of possible outcomes from any action. At the molecular level the universe denies order.

That was Icarus to me, refusing to do what he was told, flying as he pleased regardless of the risk. The myth does not tell us whether or not Icarus considered the fall to be worth the transgression. "A soul has to sin to be saved," wrote Fanny Howe. I like to imagine Icarus, having fallen, having lost his wings, swimming to shore, crawling up the rocks, finding his new life, no longer son of the great Daedalus, but an anonymous man, lost, far from home, ordinary but alive.

Expulsion would be reasonably considered a gamble, especially in ancient times—to risk expulsion from the social order could mean death, for outside the walls of the city lay a "wilderness," the realm of wild animals. By contrast, it's quite pleasant in a modern era to talk about the individual body working to be part of a broad system or society; in a certain kind of American life, for example mine, one goes to yoga classes and talks about letting go of anger and greed while still having a well-stocked kitchen at home, and a home to stock in the first place.

So how does an individual affect the system? However small the action may be, an action can address not only the internal life of the body itself but also shift in various trajectories the way a body relates to the larger system of bodies; an action can shift the relationship of the individual body to the body of the planet itself. In each small relationship an entire universe is contained. If it's true, we're in luck. "I hear voices underneath the road," Donald Revell confides. "Whichever way I go I was once an ocean."

I feel that I keep changing forms, from one body to another, from one life to another. When I was a child in Jenpeg, we would consult the *Winnipeg Tribune*'s astronomy column each morning to see which planets were visible in the sky, where we could point our telescopes to get a look at a nebula or a comet coming through. There was a little math involved in calculating the correct trajectory for viewing from Jenpeg, around five hundred kilometers to the north. My dad did the equations while I looked up stars and planets in my astronomy book.

Later in high school and college, when I tried to continue my study of astronomy I came up hard against higher math that

I could not understand and so I did not continue. Algebra was always easy for me and calculus I could conceive, but geometry and trigonometry I could not parse.

Had I only persisted I might have learned that poetry uses some of the same intuitions and techniques as math does, and that the physicists who are trying to explain the nature of the material universe are essentially dreaming, and they're using similar strategies as poets and philosophers. Are time and space the same? Is the universe infinite or limited? What is the relationship between physical mass and energy? Physicists have a set of answers and poets have a set of answers, and these intersect and diverge marvelously.

At the smallest level, quantum mechanics seems to have been able to show that matter is sparkling and foaming with activity, that stillness is impossible, that objects become other objects, and that all matter, including light, sound, gravity, and perhaps even time itself are made of discrete and finite particles. At the vastest and most unimaginably large scale, the equations of general relativity have been able to show that time and space are a continuum, that they are part of one another, not fixed but mutable, and that they bend and shift and change relative to the position of a viewer and relative to the presence of other objects and entities.

Can both be true? They can't. The easiest way for me to try to explain why (remember, I am not a scientist) is to think about black holes—an observable astronomical phenomenon that was conceived theoretically before one was ever found. If it's true that space and time bend and shift, then mass ought to convert to energy, and moreover time and space's characteristics must invert themselves upon passing the "event horizon," the border of a black hole beyond which no feedback, light, or radiation could ever escape the black hole's gravitational pull.

But radiation has been detected, emitted from a black hole. Stephen Hawking now insists that the long-accepted notion of an "event horizon"—the boundary beyond which matter completely disappears and is unobservable, because it's beyond the affect of the universe that lies outside—is a fiction, impossible with our current understanding of quantum theory, which *could* explain the radiation emission.

What does Hawking posit in place of the event horizon? Something he calls the "apparent horizon," a point at which matter is transformed but released. Though Hawking himself admits that this theory is only a stop-gap, it has a magnificent implication: There may be no black holes. And if there aren't black holes, then what is happening *inside* stars that have collapsed? Physicists are developing various approaches, including quantum gravity and string theory, to try to understand.

Why would what happens to a collapsed star make a difference to me? Because this seems analogous to the question of what happens to the *soul* when breath leaves the body?

Jack Halberstam, whose critical interests lie in what is called "low theory"—an examination of popular culture, including animated films and screwball comedies—finds in these "small projects, micropolitics, hunches, whims, fancies" a way of explaining the many small subversive ways that heteronormative culture works to perpetuate the institutions of money and political power.

Our own artistic productions and our own forays into critically engaging with the material culture that governs our lives—whether "high" or "low"—both provide ways of thinking about this unfathomable universe and learning more about ourselves. It is the "failure" of our knowledge that impels us always to think more, think deeper, think differently.

We shouldn't be surprised that physics took two thousand years to reprise Lucretius's "swerve"—the indeterminacy of atoms that corresponds with volition in humans and animals, as described in his *De Rerum Natura*—and to arrive again at the first line of Ovid's *Metamorphosis*: that "bodies change into other bodies." There is no event horizon, and everything is "apparent," in the process of transforming from one thing to another.

Or as Donald Revell says:

> Lake Michigan is Lake Michigan.
> The fate of all beings is random and awful.
>
> I have children out there. May some of them
> Be lakes that climb into the sky and live.

VASE

Vase of rain to hold
endless dogwood blooms

How I broke myself apart
pink flowering stars

Cold May after
soul beaching shoal

Nothing more still than this
quiver to swear its share

Never still to squander
what reaches in you down

Piece by piece
I shone myself

Spilled   swindled   shorn

HUMMINGBIRD

Since sin opened the world
endless any sense

I've only the thinnest inkling
shapeless vessel pour

Spendthrift day of trumpetvine
sipped from strange and sent

Senseless civil inquiry
morning glory spent

My Life Strands

after Zhang Chun Hong

Blocks of pink stone mean it is an Arab house.

Against the ruckled bark of the oak the deep lines in my face
are photographed.

At sunrise I walk along the beach as the sky turns the sharpest
pink.

Stone stairs lead to the temple in which women are not
permitted.

On the way home my scooter skids on all the fallen leaves
and I fall.

A poet tells me she is trying to list a hundred different words
for stone.

In order to defeat the rampaging demon, Vishnu took the
form of Mohini the Enchantress to trick Shiva into giving her
a child.

I dress now only in colors of spring: new leaves, first crocus, cherry blossom.

At the foot of the temple stairs a woman named Saraswati looks up.

The figure does not dare breathe but is himself breathed.

Stone is a rain or a river, inseparable.

We bring bunches of forsythia branches inside to force them to bloom.

Nightly as I climb the stone stairs to my apartment, I pass the banana flower.

Your body trembles between incarcerations.

The church is demolished but its basement is still there buried.

Last night someone said, "Palestine goes with you."

Flying over Karachi, I think "My father is down there somewhere."

I turn in no direction but loss, the sun magnet pulling me skyward.

Once seven temples ranged along the shore; six still submerged.

Saraswati begins to climb the eighteen sacred steps to the temple.

Wind steals into me.

How lonely I am among rocks a billion years old.

I was dragged to the olive tree, scent of thyme and pepper in the air.

Snow in the air makes actual sound.

Bodies are violent and vile and refuse to submit.

I drift apart like a garlanded goddess set adrift on the river.

The aspens creak like a ship at sea.

Winds in the aspens like voices steal into me.

The next day Saraswati, released without criminal charges,
watches the priests purify the altar.

Oh mountain time send me on.

Sad as a cinder I weep like a stone.

When we stood at the glacier, I was captivated by the colors—a very dark blue, a very bright white.

With cramp-ons strapped to our shoes we negotiated the edges of the glacier, climbing along ridges and smooth valleys. We came to a promontory looking out over the wide landscape of the frozen river. Because of all the melting and refreezing, the top of the glacier is contoured like a mountain range in miniature, complete with peaks and valleys, deep blue crevasses and soaring pinnacles. For a moment it is like I am still in Uttarkhand, staring out at the sun rising over the Himalayas.

Through the valleys and peaks of the constantly forming and re-forming glacier, we hear creaks and giant cracks as far beneath the surface the ice shifts and changes position.

Every part of this glacier is every other part, I realized.

Every time and place exists inside one human body.

All light in the world exists at the instant of its own creation.

You are neither mud of the earth nor matter of a star.

You are this silver road advancing, you are the man climbing aloft upon it.

You are a myth, you are music, you are a meeting place.

KAZIM NOT I AM KAZIM KNOT
COSMONAUT I AM NAUGHT NOT I AM
A KAZIMNAUT

∽

THE STARS I SEE EXIST IN DIFFERENT SPACE THAN I DO, their well-known patterns dependent on my position on the earth and their mythical associations dependent on my relationships to the stories they tell. But they exist in a different time than I: they are echoes only, of a past more remote than can be accounted for in the existence of our species, or for some of them, the existence of our planet.

"Planet" derives from a word meaning wanderer, and we are wanderers too, not just in our own lives but in a very wide universe. Existence can be an astrological practice of looking at bodies, events, and phenomena from the vantage of all space and time, in our own lives and far before them, to determine the course of action in the present moment.

Whether kismet or karma, action creates present condition. Present action creates future condition. A poem is way of mapping these directions in the present (lyric) moment. Poem as yoga asana, poem as astrological chart, poem as spread of tarot cards, poem as yelp.

This past month, the month of Janus who looks both ways, I tried to think of poetry, awareness, the human body in many different terms: conceptual art, yoga, quantum physics, Vedanta, snake oil medicine, quack science since borne out as proven, hard science since borne out as quack.

I have no defense except what Emily Dickinson wrote in her own defense: "the sailor cannot see the North—but knows the Needle can—."

To sit in the quiet of the woods and allow the earth to enter you.

To look skyward and read the ancient letters, since gone out, but when, you cannot know.

To wonder, as the weather systems of the planet itself shift and change, when will this change in the sky portend a similar change in the rocks and water table beneath. We float so lightly on the surface of what we call "continents."

My ambition to know outstrips my math but I do know how to think hard, and I have a weakness that is a strength which is that I can't make up my mind. It's an untidy place, ramshackle and unmade.

There are two genderqueer gods in the Indian pantheon. One is Ayappan, whom I mentioned before. His father was Shiva and his mother Vishnu, who had taken a female form. But there is another, Ardhanarishvara, a composite god comprised of half Parvati, half Shiva—s/he is meant to represent all creative energies of the universe.

It is as if only by choosing queerness, only by leaving behind the normative and learned patterns and looking anew at the world, one might gain understanding. This lesson is taught in the Yoga Sutra, and this path was the one pursued by Einstein and the physicists who followed him, discerning first the principles of relativity and then those of quantum mechanics and now the new theories that seek to reconcile the differences.

When I was in Varnasi during the festival called the Saraswati Puja I rejoiced, because Saraswati, consort of Brahma, is said to be still active in the world while he sleeps. She guides all wisdom-seekers, and so her festival is celebrated in particular by college and university students preparing for their exams. It is a riotous occasion. The students construct effigies of Saraswati out of twisted reeds and then process down to the river Ganges accompanied by huge speakers and strobe lights mounted on the backs of rickshaws pounding out a scintillating club mix. It's nothing less than a god-drunk traveling rave.

Two years later during the Puja, when I found myself in Kerala reading about the woman named Saraswati climbing the sacred steps of the Ayappan Temple to offer worship (and by gender supposedly defiling the place), I knew I was witnessing the true seeking of wisdom.

The myths and stories we are given, all of them, are not

about restraint and control, but about daring the consequences of thinking *past* the known: Icarus falling from the sky, Lot's wife turning back to look at the burning city, or Hanuman taking a wild leap into space to protect and rescue his friends.

Stars from different places appear to guide us. New scraps and poems from Sappho come. The slow and silvered labor of scholars reveal Emily Dickinson's ornithoid orthography, as meanings unfold themselves in enveloped stanzas.

A poet has language, its signposts and meanings, but also more importantly has body and breath to shape the experienced moment. The sculptors of ancient stone at Mahabalipuram knew this somehow, wrote the awareness into stone.

Now theoretical physicists are suggesting the possibility that the entire universe is a virtual simulation that we are inside. This is not new knowledge. Certainly Sappho, when she wrote, "someone in some future time / will think of us" had some inkling of her future life past the body, a future life *as* text.

We do transform matter into energy, energy into matter, not just at the moments of our birth or our death but in our everyday lives. That's the secret snake oil that doctors know, and mad prophets as well. Every human changes from one gender to another using an influx of hormones—this is called puberty. But Tiresias the prophet wanted to see both sides of life and so she kept switching—every seven years a new gender, a new way her body could be in the world. That was the source of her prophetic abilities, not her blindness, as certain scholars wished you believed.

And gender, like genre, is just a word to describe a set of perceptions, and it's a weak word at that, not very definitive, not very ancient—meaning tied into the system of meanings by associations of millennia—not a word like "poem" or "poetry," which eschews even those small ways of categorizing bodies or texts.

Among my own false claims was that there are more cells in the human body than there are stars in the universe. Who knows if that's true? I don't. But I *was* told yesterday that there are more bacteria in the human body than there are actual human cells. How about that? We aren't even *bodies*—we're just constellations of matter and energy and foreign presences.

So maybe Stephen Hawking is right, not just about distant phenomena such as black holes but about our lives as well. Maybe there aren't "event horizons," there are only "apparent horizons." Isn't the body itself a horizon, a shifting position that is described in process, not a locus in and of itself? If so, how can you say *Cogito ergo sum?* Who thinks?

A new poem of Sappho's has arrived just in time. It is one of two, the first Sappho texts discovered in a hundred years, recently revealed by a collector to a scholar. In a prayer for her sea-faring brother, here translated by Oxford papyrologist Dirk Obbink, the poet prays for her brother's health, but with an odd approach:

Just send me along, and command me
To offer many prayers to Queen Hera
That Charaxus should arrive here, with
His ship intact,
And find us safe.

She does not only pray for *his* safe return, but that the *family* be found safe by him. First, this speaks to how important to the life of the family this brother is, and secondly the poem puts Charaxus in the subjective position. How kind, that the most ancient of our poetry is a prayer of hope for the well-being of our siblings. That all the matter in the universe wants us to find our way safely home to be with the people who love us.

To make a body into another body is a dangerous proposition that involves crossing unimaginable horizons.

And every year sharp green spring wants to break through and alarm the new body. Who was I, a lonely boy in the Canadian north just dying to know? When I held the felt up to the snowy sky I wanted to see.

When I write a poem or practice yoga I too am Saraswati slowly transgressing, climbing the sacred steps to defile that "event horizon," that threshold or barrier at which point we are supposed to disappear.

Something else happens, something we have not approached yet, the apparent horizon. I begin to research plane tickets, scheduling my trip back to Jenpeg. What will I find there?

God is a mirror or a lens or a flensing.
This early ego, this erstwhile ersatz *ergo*.
I am nothing if not you.
Come safe home then.
Cross every border.
Become.

ACKNOWLEDGMENTS

Thank you to Jim Schley, Marie Gauthier, and Jeffrey Levine and all at Tupelo Press. Thanks to Sondra Loring and to Professor Rob Owen of the Department of Physics and Astronomy at Oberlin College. The phrase "I am was" (in the poem "All Ways to Know") is from Summi Kaipa.

Thank you to Genji, thief of strings.

I am sincerely grateful to Oberlin College for granting me research status during the 2016–2017 academic year, which enabled the completion of this book.

Earlier versions of the essays appeared on the Poetry Foundation website (www.poetryfoundation.org) as a blog during the month of January 2014, and several of the journals and prose poems appeared in *Bending Genre* and *–Esque* and on *Literary Hub* (lithub.com). "A Cartography" appeared in *Orion* and "Dome of the Rock" appeared in *Taos*.

OTHER BOOKS FROM TUPELO PRESS

See our complete list at www.tupelopress.org